HAIKU
MAMA

HAIKU
MAMA

(because 17 syllables is all
you have time to read)

by Kari Anne Roy
illustrated by Colleen O'Hara

QUIRK BOOKS
PHILADELPHIA

To Samuel Lucien and his exceptional daddy, Steven

Library of Congress Cataloging in Publication Number: 2005932894
ISBN: 1-59474-109-3
Printed in Singapore

Typeset in Rotis Semi Serif
Designed by Karen Onorato
Illustrations by Colleen O'Hara

Distributed in North America by Chronicle Books
85 Second Street
San Francisco, CA 94105

10 9 8 7 6 5 4 3 2 1

Quirk Books
215 Church Street
Philadelphia, PA 19106
www.quirkbooks.com

INTRODUCTION

You don't have time to read an introduction. You don't even have time to notice your shirt is on inside out. But these strange little poems need some explanation, so give the kids one of your looks, hold up your finger in that "gimme one second, *one second*!" pose they know so well, take a seat at the kitchen table, and read the introduction. You'll be glad you did.

This dainty little book filled with dainty little poems is not dainty at all. It does not celebrate the magical, mysterious mamahood that is found in other books of this sort. Within the pages that follow, you'll find references to poop, stretch marks, and fits of rage. You'll discover tiny little poems about the stuff no one warns you about when you become a parent. For instance, I had absolutely no idea my baby would have a smell. I mean, of course I knew he wouldn't be born smelling like baby powder, but I didn't realize he'd have his own . . . scent. And that I would love it so much. No one ever said anything about the grunting, either. Before you had one of your own, did you know that tiny babies grunt like pigs? It's awesome.

One day I decided to start documenting these weird, cute, and sometimes disturbing things babies do. I wanted to write it all down so I would never forget. But finding time to fill out a baby book was impossible. Instead, I jotted down haiku. Seventeen syllables to describe my kiddo's latest rainbow-colored diaper deposit—perfect!

As my son grew from newborn to infant to toddler, the haiku transformed, too. They became a little more sardonic, self-deprecating, and self-conscious. How can seventeen syllables explain the nervousness you feel at approaching another mom and asking her and her child out on a playdate? How do you express the dismay you feel when your one-year-old shuns his birthday cake? How do you—for the love of all that is holy—stop writing haiku about excrement?

The poems took on a life of their own. And after collecting approximately eight gazillion of these snarky little verses, I was struck by the irony of using this ancient Japanese form of poetry to document my child's newest tricks (and my own burgeoning insanity). After all, haiku is a simple, calming, poetic form meant to celebrate the glories of nature. It's quiet and respectful—like the literary version of green tea.

But having a baby—well, that's more like pounding a couple shots of peppermint schnapps: the histrionics, the noise, the violent wailing, the vomit.

When you become a mama, balance and order are buried under diapers and panic attacks. You read books upon pamphlets upon discussion boards upon scratchings on bathroom walls in search of a smidgen of something, *something*, to affirm that you're making the right decisions. But then you'll ignore your mother's advice, listening instead to DAVIDSCUTEMOMMY666 on an online message board. Yes, there is a perverse irony in detailing mama-chaos with such simple, restrictive poetry. If anyone is familiar with perverse irony, is it not a mama?

So throw this book in the bathroom. Keep it on the carefully baby-proofed coffee table. Leave it next to the rocking chair. Stow it by the breast pump. And when you have five seconds, take a peek inside. Revel in empathy. Laugh at poop jokes. And understand, for real and for true, that no mama is perfect.

This is haiku for real mamas.

This is haiku for you.

Sniffing newborn's head,
a primal urge takes over—
try not to eat him.

Hands clenched, smile subtle—
planning world domination,
or dreaming of boobs?

Snort, cough, or chortle;
the miracle of laughter
melts a mama's heart.

Forty thousand pounds:
How much stuff one baby needs;
afternoon car trip.

Outing compromised.
Small timeframe, much flatulence;
deja poo from babe.

Screaming starts to fade.
Small babe so tired, yet still weeps
melan-colic-ly.

Awake so early,
small boy rises with the sun.
Can't snooze a baby.

Note for new mama:
Falling asleep during sex?
It's forgivable.

Baby hair barrettes:
Only way to make them work
Is with duct tape, glue.

Don't tell anyone,
but it is true that if you
drop them, babies bounce.

Flickering bright lights;
sound and stories called "movies."
They still exist, right?

Shouting things in car
Look! A windmill! Look! A cow!
Is weird sans baby.

G-rated road rage,
Vocabulary yoga—
"Eat grits, turkey leg!"

A pot on the head,
a shoe on both the small hands.
So young to dress self.

Time to prune back toys:
They grow up walls like ivy,
infiltrate crannies.

It's been two full days.
Shoes are nowhere to be seen.
Can you flush sneakers?

O, lovely naptime.
You are better than birthdays
with the gifts you bring.

Wet yellow feathers—
they fall out when they dry off;
Big Bird's potty-trained.

Interest waning;
how do you up the ante
for solo pooping?

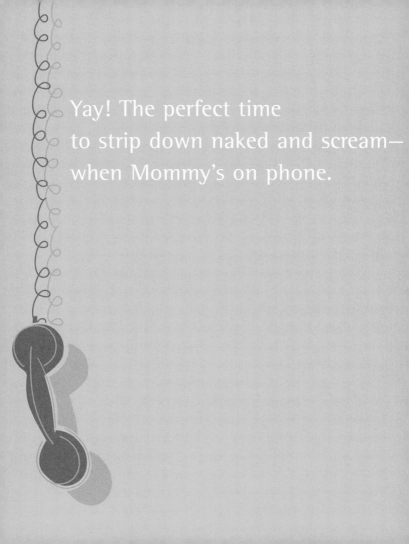

Yay! The perfect time
to strip down naked and scream—
when Mommy's on phone.

Saying "excuse me"
loses its effectiveness
when shouted ten times.

So very thankful
mascara, play sand, and ants
are all nontoxic.

Learning the "mom look":
Squint eyes, frown mouth, point finger.
But try not to laugh.

Organic panic:
air, food, water, clothing, toys;
it is all deadly.

Keep hands to yourself,
try not to breathe at daycare,
a germy minefield.

Trying to stay clean.
Warm, gray water, treacherous:
Avoid baby pool.

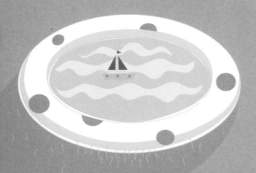

Swing set has no brakes.
Revelation to small child
as he's kicked in mouth.

Hot Story Time Mom
has cute hair, handbag. Yet has
Children of the Corn.

Bird poops on her head.
Take that, you playground bully!
Ah, schadenfreude.

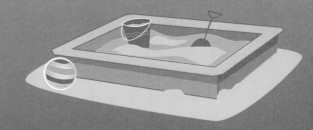

Suburban kid names:
Ryder, Hunter, Lodger, Bam.
These are not made up.

Why the funny look?
Color of baby's poopies
not fascinating?

Is it the lighting
that turns Mama into a
crazed Wal-Mart harpy?

Oh, photographer,
your misshapen, squeaky mouse
is freaking him out.

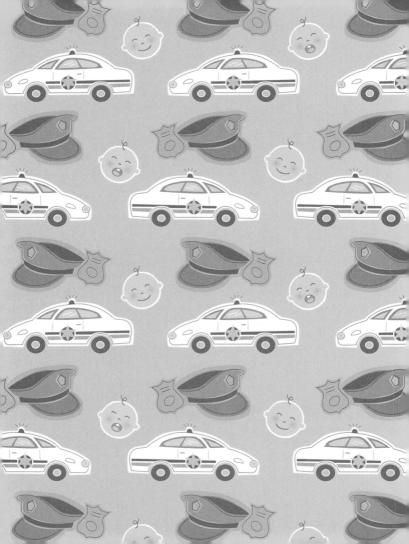

Off with a warning;
even police officers
are scared of babies.

Checking butt for worms.
Woo, the glamour never stops.
Parasites: not cool.

Innocent cashmere
attacked by flying vomit.
Free child to good home.

A magnetic draw,
begging new shoes to stomp, splash.
Thanks, fetid puddle.

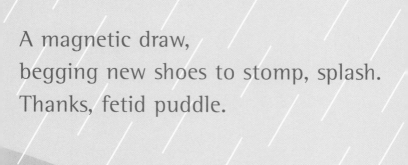

Textured wall upgrade
not really worth the money
filled with finger paint.

Stranger sees shiner.
Please do not call the police:
Babe thinks he can fly.

Bathtime is over
when more water is on floor
than still in the tub.

Does he have glove on?
Why is it writhing like that?
Oh crap, those are bugs.

Stabby curtain rod
poorly hidden in closet
is toddler's new toy.

Poor refugee dog,
his post-baby demotion
is quite unwelcome.

Toddler lexicon:
"Mommy, my butt is sneezing."
Translate that one fast.

Bubbles are awesome,
but don't pop them with your eyes.
Then they kind of suck.

Great to be mama.
One crucial thing you miss, though:
closed-door pottying.

Can't remember keys,
lunch, or where remote is, yet
Nemo? Memorized.

Same book twenty times:
comforting for the baby,
not so much for Mom.

Seuss, Seuss, such a goose
Read rhymes all day, and you'll say:
"Fried, fried, brain has died."

Maybe like chicken?
Salty, moist, melt in your mouth?
How does roast beast taste?

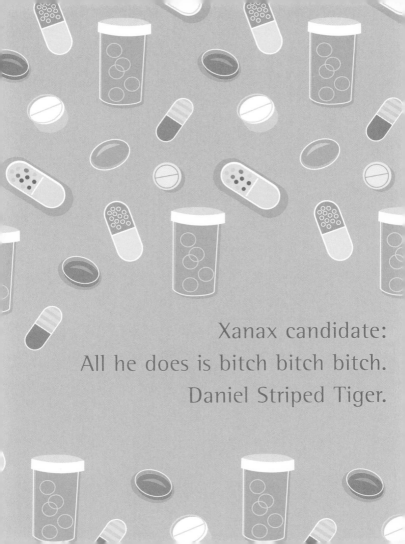

Xanax candidate:
All he does is bitch bitch bitch.
Daniel Striped Tiger.

Teletubbie fun.
Worn down like pebble in stream.
Still hate Barney, though.

Time to admit it:
Tickle him right out window—
Elmo just plain bugs.

Demands of Clifford
not met while Mommy's on phone.
Consequences dire.

Glowing tube of boobs,
you are not babysitter.
(But really, you are.)

Child hugging TV
should probably not be your
Christmas card this year.

Important lesson:
Even without batteries
remote will not float.

Mops, brushes, poison.
Cleaning house sucks donkeyballs
and dries out your hands.

Snot on monitor
gives things a nice soft focus
until it flakes off.

A new universe
begets strange new forms of life
in lost sippy cup.

Rockin' Raspberry:
Why not just call it "psycho
killer carpet stain?"

Think of it this way:
Peer pressure is not so bad
when it involves peas.

It's the newest craze:
Only eat things that are beige,
drive Mama insane!

That spaghetti squash
does not resemble pasta
or fool two-year-old.

Don't make baby's mouth
into an airplane hangar;
food will just fly out.

Can someone invent
boogers, bugs that are made of
broccoli or peas?

Just can't suck it up.
Even with moonroof, leather,
minivan be damned.

Glorious nectar,
I hardly remember thee:
vodka martini.

Moon landing, the bomb.
Not as impressive as when
husband cooks dinner.

A dirty secret:
Watching him vacuum, quite the
aphrodisiac.

A playground yeti,
he makes furtive appearance:
stay-at-home daddy.

Tennis ball in sock:
sad yet apt description of
post-nursing boobies.

When child at breast says,
"I have crunchy bunny teef,"
it's *très* alarming.

Just don't understand—
it's not supposed to be green;
breast "milk" not breast "slime."

Arms are getting buff;
have found secret for fitness—
lift fat babe, repeat.

Small, like fresh ham steak.
Get good look before it's gone;
shrinking mama butt.

Wrong to eat bagel,
Sour Patch Kids, green tea for lunch
but damn it tastes good.

Other playgroup moms,
so svelte in their yoga pants
while I eat cupcake.

Making a playdate:
Why does it feel like high school?
Fear of rejection.

Chocolate beckons;
too old for trick-or-treating,
right age for stealing.

Can't make an escape.
Could just leave him at party;
Fake aneurysm.

Screaming, crying, puke;
yelling, threats, then just chaos.
Great birthday party.

Red leaves on the trees,
glitter poop in the diaper—
it's the holidays!

Where the sun don't shine
is where you should stick foul mouth,
weird mall Santa Claus.

Wild windy weather:
stroller becomes flying kite—
aerial baby.

Dirt, dust, chicken stick;
cornucopia of spring
in belly button.

No, no, small black dog!
Your scary freakshow shedding
ruins mac and cheese.

Water-skiing . . . fun.
Unless by "skis" you mean "tires,"
and "fun," "hydroplane."

Hyper-exhaustion
sounds like an oxymoron
unless you are two.

One napless baby
plus premenstrual mama
makes raging melee.

Please grocery lady,
don't make him eat the free ham.
He is scared of you.

Never would have guessed
hairy backseat French fries are
still digestible.

Like badge of honor
our spreading hips unite us:
asstacular moms.

Two moms talk on phone;
a hint of desperation
to not speak of poop.

Shouting about it
Defies the point of teaching
the "library voice."

"Whining" and "why-ning";
very different ways to
make Mama insane.

When she was my mom
she said no sweets before lunch.
Hypocrite grandma.

ACKNOWLEDGMENTS

I've always wanted a page like this—mostly for passive-aggressive retribution against mean old professors who said I was "too creative for my own good." But karma's a bitch, so I'm not gonna do that. Instead I want to acknowledge one very special teacher, Miss Kathleen Barron. As my fifth grade reading teacher, she introduced me to haiku. This book is all her fault.

I'd also like to acknowledge my family and friends and everyone else who subjects themselves to my Haiku of the Day e-mail. Thanks for encouraging me (and I don't mean that sarcastically at all).

And thanks to Dan and Melissa. They actually believed people would want to read a book of mama-related haiku (and Dan did a very good job of letting me know when the poop haiku got a little out of hand).

Props to my former boss, Gay Gaddis at the Think Tank in Austin, Texas. She let me bring Sam to work for the first seven months of his life.

Thanks to everyone who visits www.haikuoftheday.com. All four of you. Y'all rock.

And, finally, thanks to Zach Braff, whose *Garden State* soundtrack has calmed my nerves, chilled out my baby, and fixed my erratic driving.

Hook 'em Horns,
Kari